FLOURISH
Grow • Thrive • Prosper

WENDI BLUM

This Visionbook belongs to:

_____

Published by:
Success Blueprint
Boca Raton, Florida

Copyright by Wendi Blum

All rights reserved. No part of this publication may be reproduced, scanned, uploaded, stored in a retrieval system, or transmitted, in any form or by any means, electronic, mechanical, photocopying, recording, or otherwise, without the prior written permission of the publisher.

ISBN: 978-0-9983082-1-0

I dedicate this process to my sons,
Daniel and Cory,
and to everyone throughout the world.
It is your birthright to be happy and free.

FLOURISH

Flourish: *verb* flour·ish \ˈflər-ish, ˈflə-rish\

Simple definition of *flourish*:
to grow well; to be healthy
to be very successful; to do very well
peace or *shalom*

1. To do or fare well; GROW
2. To grow exceptionally well; THRIVE
3. To be in a period of highest productivity, excellence, or influence; PROSPER

When a thing grows well, it flourishes. When a business flourishes, it gets good profits. Crops flourish when they grow well and yield a good harvest. When a person flourishes, they are healthy, wealthy, and happy.

Synonyms: increase, multiply, shoot up, blossom, bear fruit, prosper, thrive, grow

Declare it: *This is my year to FLOURISH!*

Flourish is an ENTIRE thought system and when used in its entirety will ENHANCE *every* area of your life.

Why I Wrote this Book

Hello, beautiful, gifted, talented friend. I am "over the moon" excited to share this book with you!

My WHY I do what I do is a BIG part of who I am today because of this program. This is the LEGACY I MUST leave in the world. It is my *Dharma*. It is my drive, my passion, my purpose.

My entire life changed less than ten years ago because of the teachings in this system. At that time life was just happening to me. Parts of my life were good and parts of my life were a complete disaster. One moment I was happy and the next I was in total despair.

Don't get me wrong, I had success in my career. I had a family that I loved and my health was good. Still something appeared to be missing. Something was just "off" and I couldn't figure it out. I have spent the last 10 years plus obsessing with figuring "it" out.

On that path, I had an acute awakening. I started asking questions. I started writing down my thoughts, ideas, insights, and revelations. I started mapping out goals. I became certified in NLP (Neuro-Linguistic Programming), Hypnotherapy, and Yoga. I incorporated a daily meditation practice. I studied with Marianne Williamson and other spiritual masters. I practiced. I prayed. I listened. I began to start my day by setting intentions. I experimented, put metrics in place and was I was BLOWN away!

I stumbled on success but in a WHOLE new way. Success took on a whole different meaning. Success became defined as a "FEELING." I feel good. I feel happy. I feel peaceful. I feel SUCCESSFUL. I feel whole and complete. Nothing missing.

Along the way I filled up dozens of notebooks, scratch pieces of papers, calendars, planners and index cards with the instructions (some just came as aha moments out of thin air: aka, Higher power, Creator, Source, GOD).

I HAD to put them into a SYSTEM that could be shared with my coaching clients, students and the world. One place for all of it while including space for you to add YOUR own insights, thoughts, and ideas (aka; your communication with your own Higher Power, Creator, Source, GOD).

My WHY is BIG and I know yours is too. Your WHY is my WHY.

Love is your destiny. Peace is your destiny. Living a life you love (and co-create) is your destiny.

XO, Wendi

Where Am I?

Flourishing (above the line)

Smiles Often
Collaborates
Filled With Peace
In Community
Trusts
Stretches Beyond Expectations
Open
Willing
Laughs
Grows
Tries New Things
Writes Goals
Develops Good Habits
Loving
Speaks with Confidence
Gentle
Free Spirited
Strong
Courageous
Generous
Adventurous
Holds Oneself Accountable
In Flow
Practices Excellence
Relaxed

Diminishing (below the line)

Holds Back
Distrusts
Complains
Resists Love
Makes Excuses
Overwhelmed
Frowns
Watches Hours Of Television
Judges
Always Busy
Blames Others
Compares Themselves
Lacks Sleep
Gossips
Complacent
Indecisive
Tense
Feels Stuck
Life Circumstances Define You
Bored
Uptight

Love Your Life, Rock Your Passion

Living in the Moment

Most of us are either thinking in the past or projecting into the future.

Because we think an average of 70,000 thoughts and most of them are thoughts about everything BUT the present moment—that very moment that we are living right now it completely would make sense that most of us feel "out of sorts."

Aha moment: We are "out of" the moment; of course that feels "off."

Personal pain and suffering are created in the mind by identifying with the past—or longing for the future—instead of just being in the moment. When we learn to redirect our mind, we become observers of it instead of victims of it. The Flourish system helps you learn how to redirect your mind, reframe your thoughts, and enjoy each moment as if it were your very last.

Being in the moment helps us access our creativity, our joy, and our true power.

Thought: Can you slow down time? You actually can. Remember when you were a child and time seemed to go so slowly? It seemed like forever for the last week of school to go by right before summer or leaving on family vacation. The reason is because children live in the moment. Don't you remember every detail of an ant or the leaf on a tree. Your senses were fully present, aware, and activated. You can choose to live that way again.

Power of the Subconscious Mind

Your subconscious mind is like a huge memory bank. Its capacity is unlimited. It permanently stores everything that ever happens to you. By the time you are an adult you have billions of files and information stored in this important part of your mind. It controls your deepest emotions, your habits and your perception of the world.

The function of your subconscious mind is to store and retrieve information. It only responds (reacts) by the way you are programmed. Your subconscious mind makes everything you say and do fit a pattern consistent with your self-concept formed from the time your were born (or before).

Your subconscious mind is subjective. It does not think or reason independently; it merely obeys the commands it receives from your conscious mind.

Just as your conscious mind can be thought of as the gardener, planting seeds, your subconscious mind can be thought of as the garden, or fertile soil, in which the seeds germinate and grow. Every seed that has every been planted (aka: a thought) has been planted into your garden (subconscious mind).

Your conscious mind commands and your subconscious mind obeys. This is important as we move into the Flourish system on the pages to follow. Every thought, idea, and word you write down in this book will be planted into your garden (your future). You will also be recording your words so that they can be planted deeply into your subconscious mind. You will feel resistance to it. That is normal. (That is why along with this book we include online and in person book clubs and mastermind groups.)

Conscious Mind – 10%
- Analyzes and Evaluates
- Thinks, Plans, and Reasons
- Short-term Memory

Subconscious Mind – 90%
- Habit Patterns and Addictions
- Emotions and Feelings
- Long-term Memory
- Involuntary Reflexes
- Creativity
- Intuition
- Dreams

The subconscious mind likes familiar information and will resist anything new or foreign to it. Therefore for you to grow a new garden you have to be willing to feel awkward and uncomfortable doing new things the first few times. If it's worth doing well, it's worth doing poorly until you get a feel for it; until you develop a new comfort zone at a new, higher level of competence. It's all about getting deep into the subconscious mind.

Love Your Life, Rock Your Passion

Brainwaves States

What are they and why are they important to understand?

At the root of all our thoughts, emotions and behaviors is the communication between neurons within our brains. Brainwaves are electrical pulses produced from our neurons communicating with each other.

Brainwave speed is measured in Hertz (cycles per second) and they are divided into bands delineating slow, moderate, and fast waves.

Why is this important? Because thoughts, ideas, and information received during certain brainwave states have more power than during other times. The impulse (signal) can go deeper into the subconscious mind at higher brainwave states.

We also release brain chemicals based on our "feelings." Serotonin is released when you feel good and cortisol is released when you feel stressed. All of this affects the information processing systems deep within our mind.

Our goal is to reach a higher brainwave state (induced with hypnosis, meditation, walking in nature, painting, and listening to our recordings in the Flourish system). The reason that the Flourish system induces a "feel-good" state is that the subconscious mind does not know if something is real or imagined—therefore it will imprint a vision as the powerful seed as if it has already happened. The mind then accepts it as already done, releasing even more serotonin into our bloodstream and grows the mind strong in belief, since it has accepted the vision as complete.

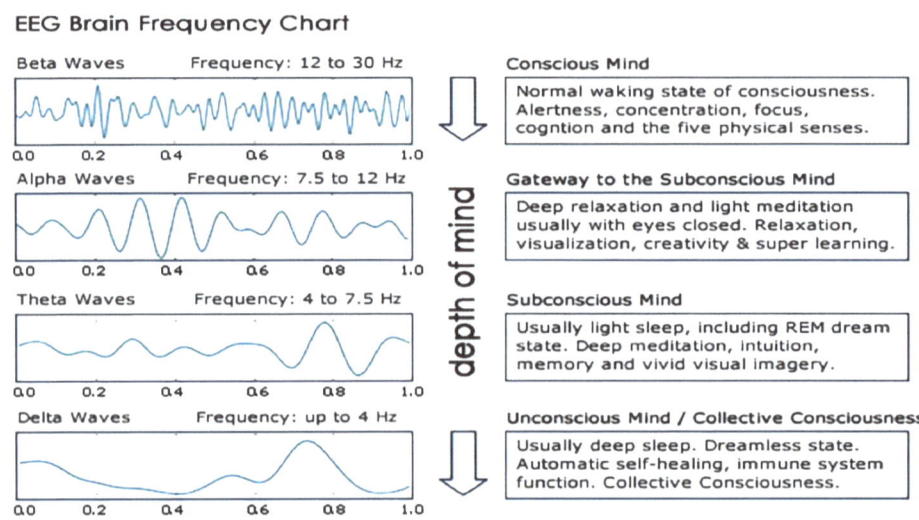

What Is Success?

Whatever you're thinking about is like planning for a future event.

When you're doubting, you are planning.

When you are grateful, you are planning.

What are you planning?

COMMITMENT

I, _____ (insert your name here), am worthy and it is my birthright to live a life I love, period. I am finally ready to commit to (free flow it, baby):

_____
_____
_____
_____
_____
_____
_____
_____
_____
_____
_____
_____
_____
_____

THE PROMISE YOU MAKE TO YOURSELF IS THE MOST IMPORTANT ONE YOU WILL EVER MAKE!
(JUST SAYIN')

Questions: Getting Real

Where am I right now?

You need to review your goals on a regular basis (quarterly, monthly, or weekly). If you haven't taken any steps toward accomplishing a certain goal for several weeks or months, then there might be something blocking your goal. Go back to your list of desires and get clear on your BIG why before pursuing it any further.

How much progress have I made?

It's important to measure success along the way. You will want to monitor your progress and decide along the way if you need to change or modify your approach. Deadlines keep you accountable. It is helpful to break larger goals down into smaller mini goals. If you get sidetracked or fail to reach a goal, you have powerful information so that you can adjust your mini goals leading to the bigger stretch goals.

What are my strengths?

You need to have the right skills to obtain many of your goals. Break individual skills down into action steps (i.e., a smaller goals) that are part of the bigger ones. For example, if you wanted a new profession (stretch goal), you may need a certification or a specific training, which then becomes a mini goal that leads to the new career.

How flexible am I?

Your goals must not be in conflict with each other. As you progress with one goal, it may influence some other goal, so you need to be prepared to constantly revise your plan. Be agile and quick to make changes, and it will serve you in the long run.

Questions: Exploring

What are my heart's deepest desires?

Your goal must be something that is valuable and is a priority in your life. When you have a burning desire then you are willing to take the necessary actions steps to make it happen.

What if?

Larger and worthwhile goals take time. You need to be consistent and willing to put forth the effort to keep progressing toward your goals. Once you achieve an individual goal (high fives), continue the same momentum forward toward your next goal.

How do I celebrate?

It's all about the journey, not really the destination. Life is about having experiences that are rich and fulfilling. Take time along the way to high five, dance, and celebrate! Add seven ways you celebrate below. (A few of mine are dancing, travel, going out to dinner, having friends over, etc.)

1. _____
2. _____
3. _____
4. _____
5. _____
6. _____
7. _____

The Power of Desire

Write out one wish or more that you have for yourself.

1. _____
2. _____
3. _____
4. _____
5. _____
6. _____
7. _____
8. _____
9. _____
10. _____
11. _____
12. _____
13. _____
14. _____
15. _____
16. _____

Feelings & Emotions

Release	Replace With
Denial	Belief
Doubt	Confidence
Entitlement	Gratitude
Fear	Love
Feeling Closed	Open Heart
Frowns	Smiles
Guilt	Acceptance
Harsh Words	Gentle Thoughts
Judgment	Compassion
Lack	Plenty
Mistakes	Learning
Negativity	Positivity
Pain	Vibrancy, Health, Wholeness
Procrastination	Action, Achievement
Self-sabotage	Strength, Discipline, Power
Staying Stuck	Moving Forward
Selfishness	Giving
Unworthiness	Worthiness
Of the World	Of God

The Power of Belief

I believe... _that success and happiness are everyone's birthright._

I believe... _____

I believe... _____

I believe... _____

I believe... _____

I believe... _____

I believe... _____

I believe... _____

I believe... _____

I believe... _____

I believe... _____

I believe... _____

I believe... _____

I believe... _____

I believe... _____

I believe... _____

I believe... _____

I believe... _____

Stretching Your Belief Muscle

Fear versus Freedom

Identify 3 fears:

1. _____
2. _____
3. _____

IF IT'S BOTH TERRIFYING AND AMAZING,
YOU SHOULD DEFINITELY PURSUE IT.
—ERADA

What does the "Voice of Courage" say to fear?

You can do it—I know you can . . .
_____
_____
_____
_____
_____
_____

F.E.A.R. (FALSE EVIDENCE APPEARING REAL)

5 Categories

1. Purpose

2. Relationships

3. Health

4. Lifestyle

5. Love

My Big "Why"

Let's have a heart-to-heart.

You probably want to stick around (for at least another 30 to 40 years or more) so you probably want to be the happiest, healthiest version of you. So we've got some work to do!

Let's map this thing out and create a life you love.

Decide. Declare. Actualize.

* We shall set our intentions on our heart's deepest desires.

* We shall give up all remnants of guilt.

* We shall forgive ourselves and forge ahead.

* We shall overcome all of our obstacles.

* We shall move beyond scarcity, fear, doubt, or worry.

* We shall claim our happiness as our birthright.

* We shall focus on what we already have in gratitude and appreciation.

* We shall shift, expand, and raise our level of consciousness.

* We shall claim our personal power and refuse to give it away to others.

* We shall courageously step forward into our greatness.

* We shall know our worthiness and our value.

* We shall come back to home in knowing all there is is love.

Trust

THE UNIVERSE HAS MY BACK

Love Your Life, Rock Your Passion

1. Purpose

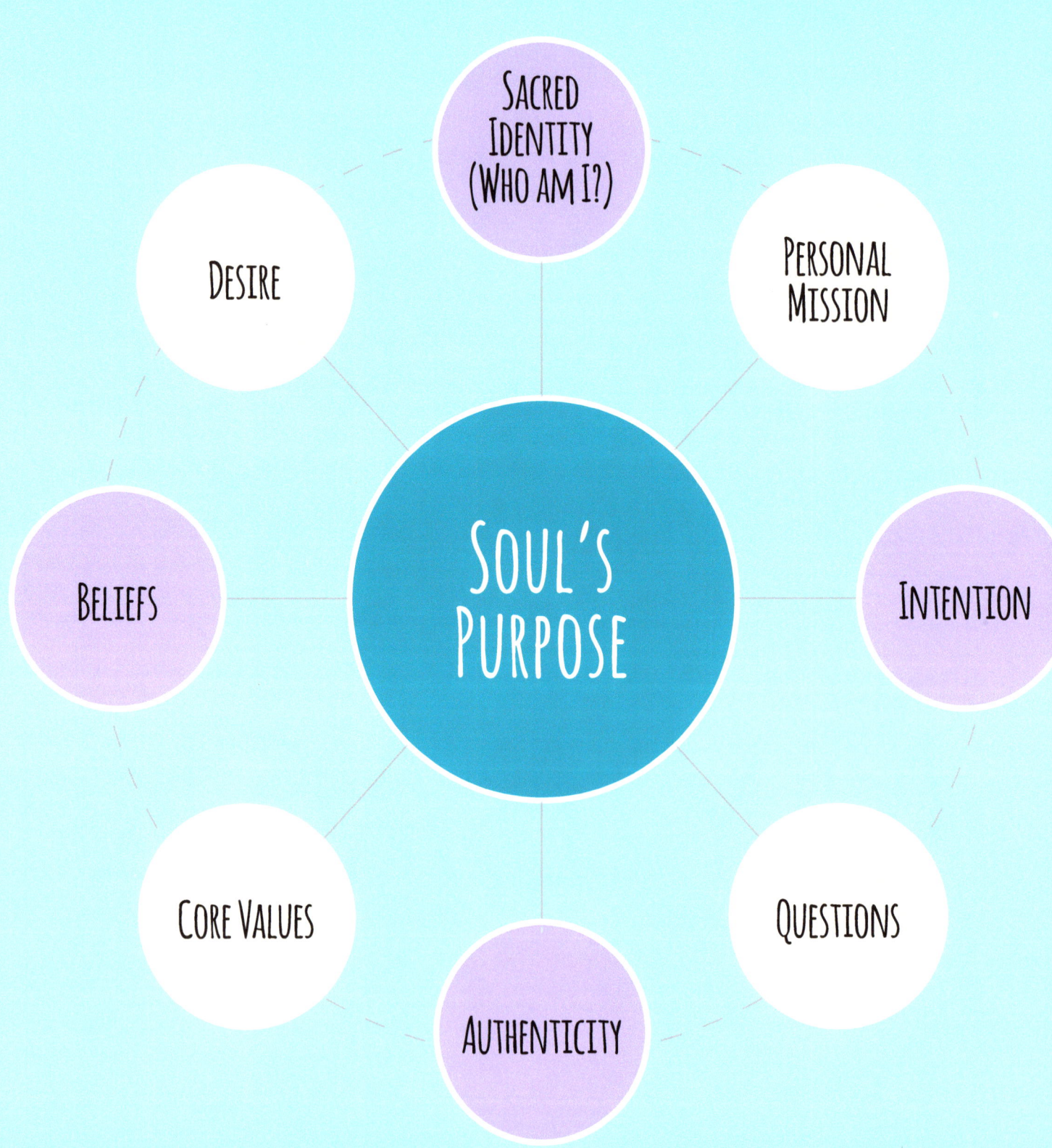

What Is Purpose?

Your soul is guiding you toward your core values, mission, and your ultimate potential. It excites you and scares you at the same time.

It is your highest goal coming from the highest very best within you.

Your purpose is the "drive forward" from your soul. It becomes your beacon of light shining your life's path forward.

It's your inspiration, your mojo, your reason to live your life. You can point to it as your compass or North Star.

Start by aligning with your highest and best emotional self. Your A list:

Happy	Kind	Disciplined	Confident
Optimistic	Loving	Empowered	Authentic
Courageous	Generous	Enthusiastic	

Add more here: _____

_____

Your life's purpose draws you in, adding something valuable into the world. It's your higher self calling you to be more than you are right now. It nudges you from inside your heart.

Start by asking these powerful questions:

Who can I help? What can I share?

What would the highest and best version of me do at this time in my life? Maybe it's to take care of your family or maybe it's to share a smile.

Your inner being knows.

It's all about allowing answers to slowly reveal themselves just being the happiest, kindest, person you can be in this moment, while starting a conversation about who you would like to become in the months/year ahead.

"My purpose in life is to love and help other people." —MOTHER TERESA

Love Your Life, Rock Your Passion

Sacred Identity (Who am I?)

When you strip away the conditioned layers of who you are (wife/husband, mother/father, daughter/son, accountant, journalist, etc.) what you are left with deep inside of you is your true essence.

Perhaps you see that you are light, you are God, you are compassion, or any identity stripped away by society's classifications.

What is your Sacred Identity? Proclaim it and live by it for your soul to flourish.

_____

_____

_____

_____

_____

Exercise: Grab a hand mirror and look closely into your eyes. See beyond your physical form and look into your soul. Go deep and search for your higher self. This may seem awkward at first, but you will sense some part of you that observes and watches over you. Connect to that part and silently speak words of encouragement like: "You have this thing," or "I have your back, don't worry." You may become teary-eyed, which only means you are connecting to your true sacred identity.

> "Identity is this incredible, invisible force that controls your whole life. It's invisible like gravity is invisible, but it controls your whole life."
> —TONY ROBBINS

Personal Mission

What do you want to accomplish for your days on this earth? What is your personal mission that will drive you forth: i.e., keep you balanced in rough seas and steady to drive forward when it is calm?

Personal Mission Statement: What have you been brought to this earth, to this universe to accomplish?

_____

_____

_____

_____

_____

_____

_____

_____

_____

_____

_____

"My mission in life is not merely to survive but to thrive; and to do so with some passion, some compassion, some humor, and some style."
—MAYA ANGELOU

Love Your Life, Rock Your Passion

INTENTIONS

To be true to your highest self and accomplish what you would like this moment, this day, this year, this lifetime it is helpful to begin each day with a positive soul-affirming intention. You can come back to this intention and use it as a mantra to guide your actions as you go through your life.

What Intentions do you want to live by? Think of *goals* as being in your mind and *intentions* as coming from your heart.

_____

_____

_____

_____

_____

_____

_____

_____

_____

"Our destiny is ultimately shaped by our deepest intentions."
—WENDI BLUM

QUESTIONS

What questions does your Soul ask? When you ponder and go deep to ask meaningful questions about life, what comes up for you?

Example: Why am I here? What is my destiny? And why, sometimes, do we suffer great loss? Is there a purpose for me?

What are your Soul's questions? How? What? When? Why?

_____

_____

_____

_____

_____

_____

_____

_____

_____

_____

*"When we let go of something that no longer serves us,
we create space for something that does."*
—WENDI BLUM

AUTHENTICITY

One of the most important things that you can do for yourself is to be TRUE to who you are. In the beginning, this many not be easy—until you truly get to know yourself. In every aspect of your life, authenticity is vital for you to be able to flourish, grow, thrive, and prosper.

Describe your Authentic Self:

_____
_____
_____
_____
_____
_____
_____
_____
_____

"I know I am being authentically me because I feel happy and free."
—WENDI BLUM

Core Values

Just as the company you work for or the society you live in has a set of core values that apply, each of us has our own core values by which we live our lives. Sure, you probably know this, but maybe you haven't thought of it in this way. You may want to ask yourself if you are living your core values in all aspects of your life.

For example, perhaps *truth* and *compassion* are two of your core values, but every now and then you catch yourself speaking negatively about someone. Remember, your core values are a guide to help you flourish. After you write them out below, review the list from time to time to keep you on track.

What are your Core Values?

_____

_____

_____

_____

_____

_____

_____

"Values are who you are when no one's watching."
—JOHN WOODEN

Love Your Life, Rock Your Passion

Beliefs

Beliefs are the way you think about things and are the underlying reason you act a certain way (which is always based on your belief system). What you believe, you actually draw more of into your experience. Our subconscious mind is always calling the shots.

Also, note that beliefs can be either positive or negative. Negative beliefs are limiting beliefs but positive beliefs take you into new possibilities of unlimitlessness.

The really cool thing about beliefs is that they CAN change. First you have to identify yours; so I invite you to go into your personal belief system and write out a few of them here.

What are your Beliefs?

_____
_____
_____
_____
_____
_____
_____

Your belief muscle can be redefined the same way your biceps are strengthened in the gym.

> *"Whether you think you can, or you think you can't—*
> *you're right."*
> —HENRY FORD

DESIRE

Deep down, what do you dream about? What would you do if you knew you could not fail? What do you want to bring forth and accomplish during THIS one beautiful life of YOURS? (Desire is your drive.)

Acknowledging your deepest desires is a powerful tool and, when identified, can be even be strengthened.

What do you Desire?

_____

_____

_____

_____

_____

_____

_____

_____

*"The starting point of all achievement is desire.
Keep this constantly in mind. Weak desires bring weak results
just as a small amount of fire makes a small amount of heat."*
—NAPOLEON HILL

2. Health

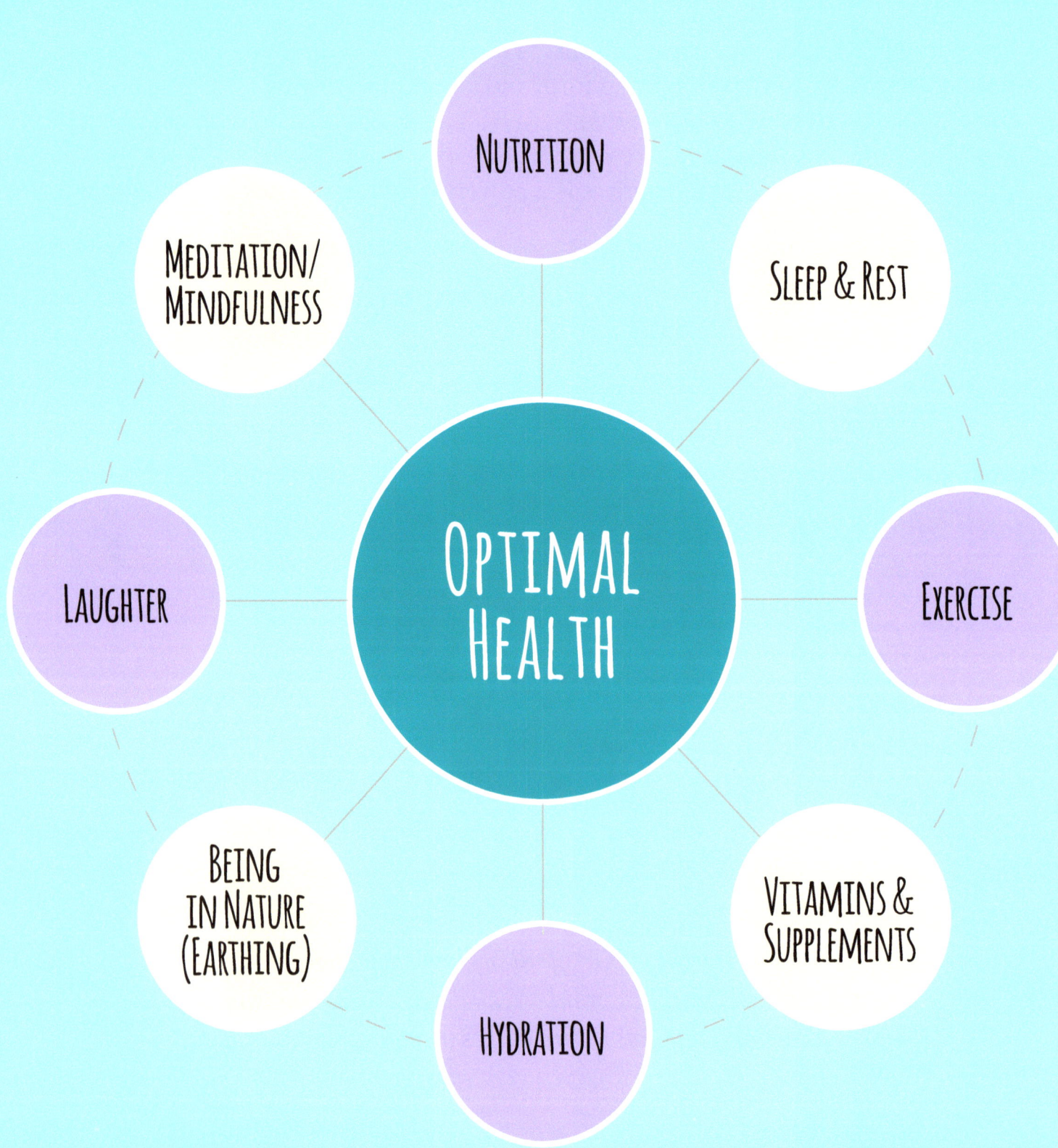

What Does Good Health Look Like?

When you see someone who is truly healthy you can see it in their eyes—their skin is radiant and glows, and their energy level is high.

What does Good Health look like to you?

_____
_____
_____
_____
_____
_____
_____
_____

You can always improve your health—it's never too late to enhance your well-being.

> *"Take good care of your body.
> It's the only place you have to live."*
> —JIM ROHN

Nutrition

The adage, "Let Food Be Thy Medicine," says it all. What you put into your body is going to dictate how you feel. A plant-based, whole-foods diet full of yummy goodness, free of pesticides and processed foods, will make you feel your best.

As an added bonus, you will look your best ever. You will also have the energy you need to power your body through this world.

On a scale of 1–10, how nutritious is your current diet? _____

What are some ideas for you to incorporate more nutritious choices into your daily schedule?

_____
_____
_____
_____
_____
_____
_____

Suggestions: Don't eat when you are in a rush, stick to the outer aisles of the grocery store, go to your local farmer's market, explore a practice such as Ayurveda (the ancient practice of eating for your specific body constitution).

Sleep & Rest

I need _____ hours of sleep each night to feel good for the next day. (And *YES!* I deserve to feel good!)

Bedtime Ritual to Enhance Deep Sleep (i.e., reading, taking a warm bubble bath, rubbing oils or lotion onto your body, putting lavender drops on your feet, listening to relaxing music):

_____

_____

_____

_____

Remember, watching the news before going to sleep imprints negative messages into the subconscious mind. Looking at electronics, including your smartphone, stimulates your mind instead of inducing rest. *Why not plant beautiful seeds for your subconscious mind instead?*

Helpful Tips: Listen to Binaural beats 528Hz high-frequency meditation music, crystal bowls, or a heart-opening gong meditation (all easily found on a service such as Spotify) to relax your mind and move into a calm and peaceful state for drifting off to sleep.

Exercise

You only have one body for this lifetime—this is it. Your body is your temple—the way that you experience this world for this lifetime. Now, I am not going to tell you something that you don't already know . . . but sometimes, we have to hear it again and again before the motivation kicks in.

So here it goes for you one more time: If you want to truly Flourish in your body it has to be strong, flexible, fit, and operating at its optimal capacity.

Exercise Suggestions for Optimal Health:

- Weights, especially to minimize bone loss.
- Yoga, for flexibility and to decrease the odds of a fracture due to a fall.
- Tennis, tai chi, golf, bike riding, running, cycling, swimming, walking, dancing, and . . . .

Add your favorites to the list here:

_____
_____
_____
_____
_____
_____
_____

What matters is what inspires you to move and be healthy.

Vitamins & Supplements

If you eat a nutritious diet, most of your vitamins should be included with your food. However, if you adhere to a certain lifestyle choice, there may be certain vitamins and supplements that you want to consider.

Suggestions: Vitamins A, B, C, D, and E; wheat grass; E3Live blue-green algae*; maca powder; cacao; chia seed; and many more. If you are a vegetarian, you will not get enough vitamin B12 from your food (important for brain health). Some people lack vitamin D3, even in sunny climates, as well as magnesium, which also contributes to brain health. These could be other helpful additions to your regimen.

Talk to a holistic/functional medicine doctor, nutritionist, or health coach for more details and information.

What are the daily vitamins and supplements you currently take?

_____
_____
_____
_____

Are there any current symptoms that you want to address by taking vitamins and supplements?

_____
_____
_____
_____

* Call 888-800-7070 for complimentary E3Live and mention *Flourish*

Love Your Life, Rock Your Passion

Hydration

Up to 60% of the adult human body is comprised of water. Health experts recommend eight 8-ounce glasses, or around a half gallon (2 liters) of water per day.

How much hydration are you getting each day?

_____
_____

What are some ways that you could up your hydration intake?

_____
_____
_____
_____
_____

Did you know that cancer doesn't survive in an alkaline environment but thrives in an acidic environment? You can purchase pH strips at your local pharmacy and check your levels.

Healthy blood has a pH level of 7.35. A pH below 7.0 is acid and is an indication of less than optimal health. You could experience symptoms like low energy, pains and aches, mood swings, worries and fears, poor sleep, or being overweight.

You can reverse this acid state by consuming alkaline water and foods. It is also recommended that you add lemon to water to balance out your pH (lemons, even though they are acidic, help to balance out your pH).

Being in Nature (Earthing)

It feels so good to be outside in **nature,** but let's face it: our generation is spending more and more time indoors, behind a screen or device.

What I know to be true is that we crave nature, and it is not only a desire but required for good health, creativity, and success!

Suggestions for you to reconnect with Mother Earth:

- Sitting under a tree.
- Going for a walk in your neighborhood.
- Walking on the beach.
- Laying down in a hammock.
- Swimming in a like or the ocean.
- Smelling flowers in a garden.
- Sitting on a bench in a metropolitan city.
- Walking barefoot in your backyard.
- Opening your windows and letting the breeze and the sound of birds inside.

List some other ways you connect with nature:

_____

_____

_____

_____

Ground yourself with nature and see the magic of the universe unfold.

Laughter

Some say that laughter is the best medicine. When you smile, even when you are talking on the phone the tone of your voice changes. How often are you letting humor into your life?

I laugh an average of _____ times a day.

Suggestions:

- Watching funny YouTube videos (pets and similar videos) make us naturally laugh.
- Tickling your spouse or children.
- Sending funny memes to your friends.

What makes you have a good belly-aching laugh?

_____
_____
_____
_____
_____
_____

"Laughter is the shortest distance between two people."
—VICTOR BORGE

Meditation/Mindfulness

We think an average of 70,000 thoughts a day and most of them repeat themselves over and over and over again in our brains. Even worse, most of them are negative.

Stillness, quiet time, and meditation allow us a momentary release of striving, of trying, and doing so we can create space in our mind.

Here's the deal: meditation can take MANY different forms.

Circle any of the activities below that appeal to you.

- Sitting in a chair.
- Closing your eyes.
- Sitting in a lotus position on the ground.
- Going for a walk quietly.
- Taking a long, relaxing shower.
- Going for a drive (Steven Spielberg created his award-winning movies on the road).
- Listening to music.
- Closing your eyes while dancing.
- Using a mantra.

Fill in other suggestions that work for you here:

_____
_____
_____
_____
_____

3. Relationships

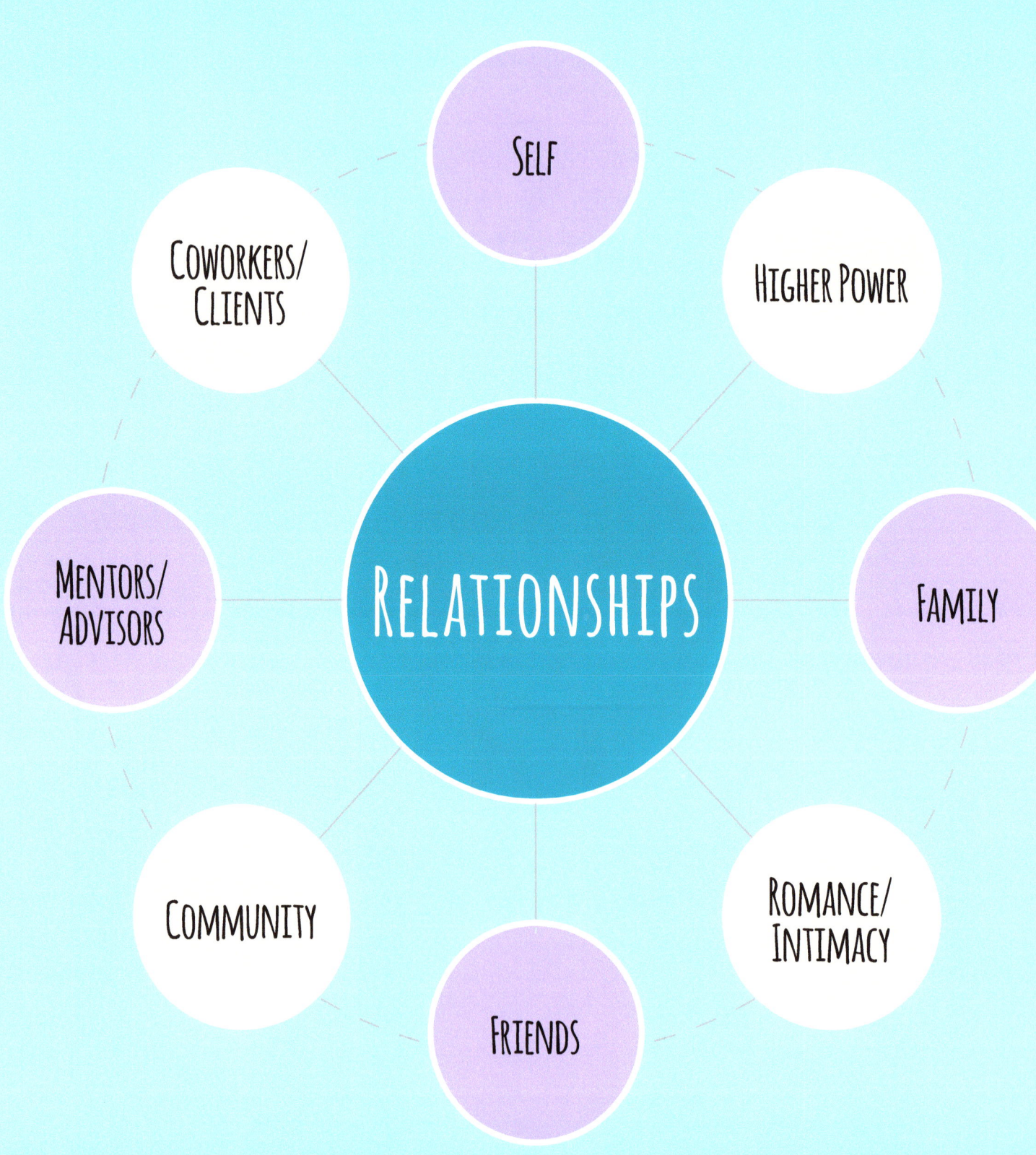

What Is a Healthy Relationship?

The most important relationship you will ever have is the relationship you have with yourself—everything else cascades out from there.

You know you're in a good relationship when you and those around you feel good.

What does a healthy relationship look like to you?

_____
_____
_____
_____
_____
_____
_____

> *"Real beauty in relationships comes from the absence of judgment of others . . . and yourself."*
> —WENDI BLUM

Self

We all know that saying "I feel like a million bucks!" Well, I have a question for you. *How valuable do you think—or believe—that you are?*

People will treat us as we treat ourselves. Self respect. Self love. Self care. They all matter. A lot.

On a scale of 1–10, how worthy are you of living an amazing life? How deserving do you feel? _____.

It is time to fall in love and have an amazing relationship . . . with yourself.

Suggestions:

- Massage
- Golf
- Spending time at the library or at a museum you love
- Meditation
- Taking an art class
- Writing or journaling
- Yoga
- Breathwork
- Taking a bubble bath

What activities do you include each week that honor that relationship?

_____
_____
_____
_____

Do whatever it is that makes your heart sing!

Higher Power

Do you believe in a Higher Power? Something greater, bigger and more expansive watching over you and the entire universe?

How often do you think about Creation and Life itself? _____
(Often, Seldom, Periodically, All the time)

On a scale of 1–10, how connected do you feel to this "Source"? _____

In what ways do you connect with this power?
_____
_____
_____
_____

Ideas:

- Prayer
- Meditation
- Intention
- Reading spiritual books such as the Bible or other religious texts
- A Course in Miracles
- Nature

In what ways could you deepen this connection?
_____
_____
_____
_____

Family

How close are you to your family? Do you feel that you could strengthen this bond?

Suggestions:
- Weekly dates
- Sunday evening dinners
- Facetime with children
- Photo sharing in the iCloud
- A family reunion

Add more ways that you could strengthen your ties to your family:

_____
_____
_____
_____

Write down a list of important birthdays or events, put them in your calendar on your iPhone, and reach out on days that matter to your loved ones.

Now to the elephant in the room. Perhaps in some cases, a grievance has materialized over the years or you have disconnected with a family member (or 2 or 3 or 4).

When you are ready to forgive someone or something of the past you create a gateway of radiant gifts to enter into your own life (*just sayin'*).

Romance/Intimacy

Long relationships, partnerships, and soulful intimacy feels incredible. We seek it out. We year to encounter it. When we enter into a union feeling whole and complete, it is then that our love relationships can truly flourish.

Use the space below to describe your ideal relationship with your wonderful boyfriend, girlfriend, husband, wife, or life partner.

_____
_____
_____
_____
_____

Use the space below to draw or to place a photo (one of your own or from a magazine) that represents the loving, happy, intimate relationship you desire.

FRIENDS

Life is meant to be enjoyed. If we had all of the riches of the world but without anyone to share them with, life would feel lonely and incomplete.

Describe your tribe, your close friends, your social circle, and then add to it and expand your vision.

Ideas:

- Musicians
- Artists
- CEO's of innovative companies
- Authors
- Athletes
- Foodies
- Movie lovers

Use the above ideas to create your list below:

_____
_____
_____
_____
_____

"Good friends, good books, and a sleepy conscience:
this is the ideal life."
— MARK TWAIN

Community

We are shaped and influenced by our community. We make decisions based on where we want to live based on location, but we are part of a bigger picture of our environment and what is going on around us.

Being a part of a community by adding to it makes us feel a deep sense of connection. We can get involved at any level we choose to and feel the benefits.

Describe the Community that you are a part of below:
_____
_____
_____
_____
_____

Add ways that you are involved or can deepen your involvement:
_____
_____
_____
_____
_____

Mentors/Advisors

Remember, success leaves a trail. Those that have traveled a similar path and have done it well feel a need to pay it forward to others hoping to follow their lead.

Know who the influencers and movers and shakers are in your industry, community, and workplace. Seek them out, and more often than not they will help to mentor you and guide you along your own path. When it is your turn, you will do the same.

Think back on who has helped you to get to where you are right now. Teachers, mentors, coaches, and guides throughout your life:

_____
_____
_____
_____
_____

Now think of the type of people to whom you are drawn at this stage of your personal and professional development:

_____
_____
_____
_____
_____

Coworkers/Clients

A large proportion of people spend the majority of their waking hours at their job, interacting with coworkers and clients. Who you surround yourself with, the atmosphere and energy that these relationships bring, and how you interact influences you.

Describe your current Office family:

_____
_____
_____
_____

Note, if there are aspects that drain you, brainstorm below how you can make it better for yourself (i.e., I recognize my coworkers like to gossip. When this happens I will shift the conversation or excuse myself to get back to my work).

_____
_____
_____
_____
_____

4. Love

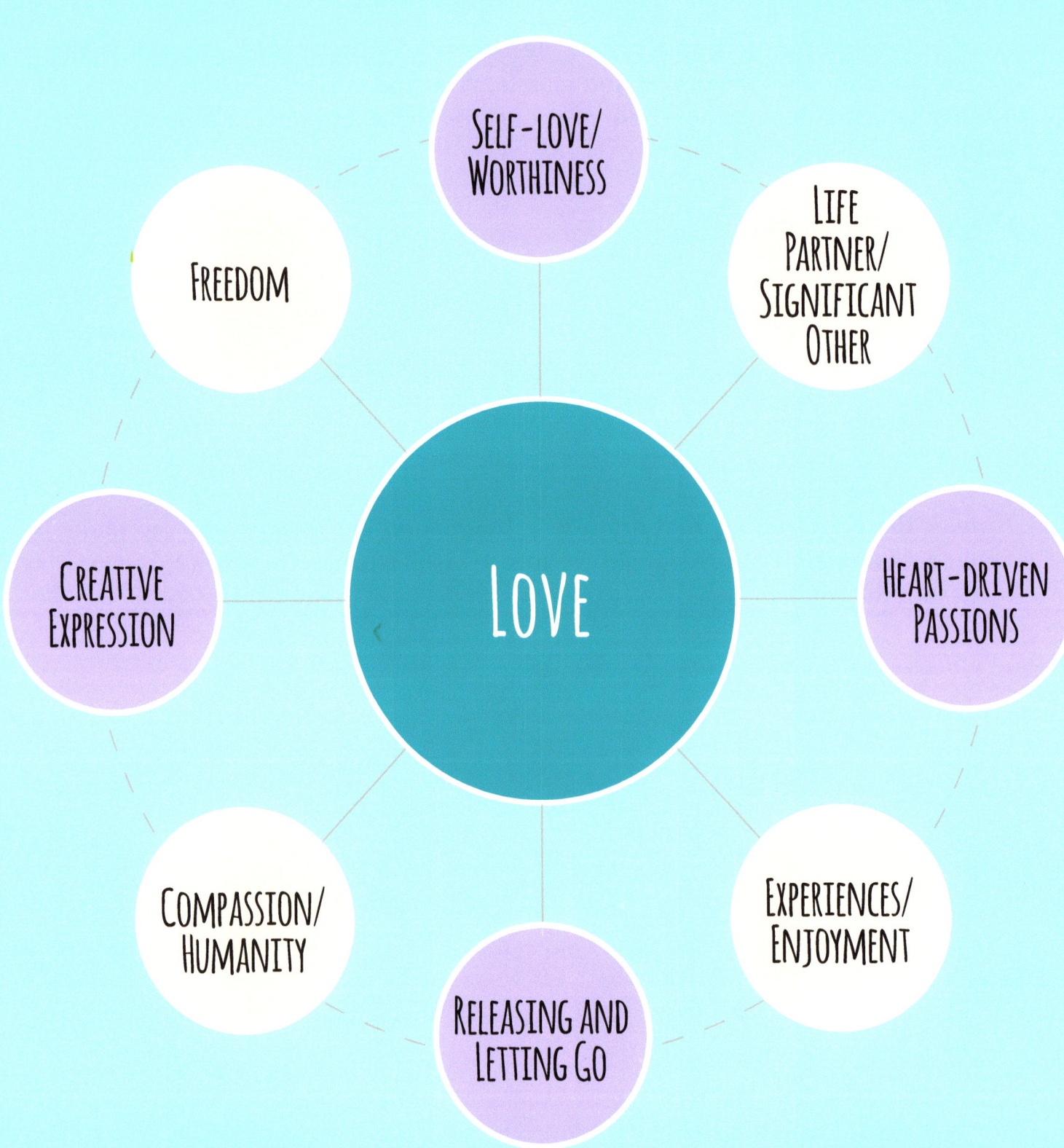

What Is Real Love?

Love is something that goes beyond the material world to something that is greater, deeper, richer, and more complete than the mind can comprehend. It's always there; it's always available to us, and we can access it anytime because it's the essence of what we are made of. As author Brian Weiss, MD, writes, only love is real.

What does real love look like to you?

_____
_____
_____
_____
_____
_____

"Love is boundless, timeless, and free-flowing all the time."
—WENDI BLUM

Self-love/Worthiness

In order to give love, first we need to fill ourselves up with love. And where does that come from?

Remember when you first laid eyes on your baby (or your niece, or your pet, or someone that you felt unconditional love for), and you instantly felt love pouring out from inside of you? Babies, especially, remind us that they are created in love—and remember—that was once YOU.

There is SO much love within us all the time, but we can't always see it. Love is an energy and it is abundantly flowing all around us and in us all of the time. We just have to be present and remember.

Declare: I am as GOD, the Universe, the Higher Power that created me. I am love. I fill myself up with so much love. I am worthy of love. I am love.

Create your own Worthiness affirmations here:

_____
_____
_____
_____
_____
_____
_____
_____

Life Partner/Significant Other

There is a Universal law that always applies: what we give away boomerangs back to us. We receive what we give out. If you want more love in your relationship, give it freely, abundantly, unconditionally, and compassionately away without comparing, questioning, or holding back.

Decision Time: You don't control anyone but yourself. People come into your life for a reason, a season or even a lifetime. You can change to be the best version of yourself, the most loving partner and the best that you can be in your relationship.

Commitment Statement. Add your own intention here:

_____
_____
_____

In my relationship, I choose to:

_____
_____
_____
_____
_____
_____

People come into our lives for a reason, a season, or a lifetime.
—ANONYMOUS

Heart-Driven Passions

What makes your heart and soul come "alive"? Instead of *IF something*, I would prefer to say: *WHEN something comes from your heart.* If something comes from your heart, because you truly care—and better yet, you can identify these passions—you will be able to do great work in this world.

What are your Heart-Driven Passions?

_____
_____
_____
_____
_____
_____
_____
_____

Experiences/Enjoyment

In what experiences do you naturally flourish? Where do you find you most feel joy?

Pinpointing the activities that bring us joy can remind us of what we need to include more of in our lives.

List some Experiences that bring you Joy:

_____
_____
_____
_____
_____
_____
_____
_____
_____

When you love life, life loves you back.
—WENDI BLUM

Releasing and Letting Go

Maybe life is teaching us to let go all of the time so that we can grow stronger and prepare for the next phase of our lives.

It is in the releasing and letting go that allows the resistance to the new to break open. Releasing is a practice and a muscle that must be developed. It isn't always easy, but in the end it is the only way you can become free (physically, emotionally, and spiritually).

Recognize below extra weight that you figuratively carry that you are ready to release.

_____
_____
_____
_____
_____
_____
_____
_____

*In the end these things matter most: How well did you love?
How fully did you live? How deeply did you let go?*
— JACK KORNFIELD, *BUDDHA'S LITTLE INSTRUCTION BOOK*

Compassion/Humanity

Without compassion for yourself and for humanity it will be hard for you to tap into deep love. Just look to the news and see how the world struggles. If you can be a ray of light and hold yourself and those you meet with compassion you will truly flourish in meaningful ways.

What is the level of Compassion that you hold for yourself?

_____
_____
_____
_____

In what ways could you evoke more compassion in the way that you interact with yourself and with the world?

_____
_____
_____
_____
_____
_____
_____
_____

Creative Expression

Whether you find it through dance, music, writing, gardening, painting, working with your hands, or cooking a meal, taking the time to creatively express yourself is an important way to release who you are to this world and also bring you joy.

What form are you drawn to when you Creatively Express yourself?

_____
_____
_____
_____
_____
_____
_____
_____

Inside of you is an artist that wants to emerge.
—WENDI BLUM

Freedom

It is said that *hope* is the only thing that is stronger than fear. To allow yourself a true canvass to tap into all of the potential that this world holds, you must be free to embrace what the universe puts on your path.

How Free and Open to new possibilities do you feel?

_____
_____
_____
_____

What would it take for you to take a leap, be it big or small, to get out of your comfort zone and truly fly and be free?

Make a list below of how you can open up.

_____
_____
_____
_____
_____
_____
_____
_____

"Manifest your own FREEDOM."
—WENDI BLUM

5. Lifestyle

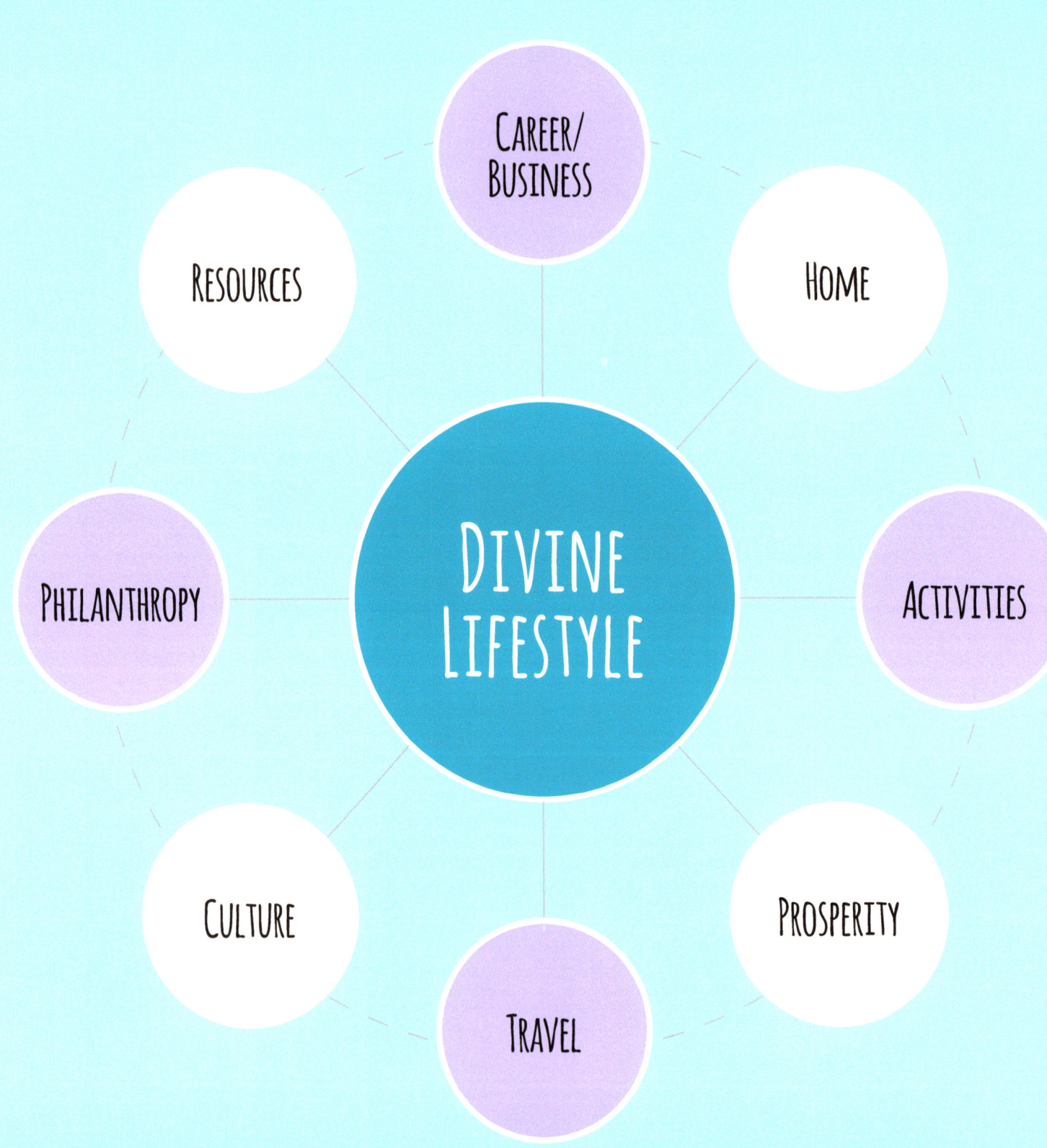

What Is Your Ideal Life "style"?

When you are surrounded by people you love, things you love, and doing things you love, you are living a divine lifestyle. Most people believe that doesn't happen until they retire, but it's available to you right now. We think of lifestyle as being something big, but it's really a collection of the small things that give you joy every day.

Lifestyle includes healthy eating, living your purpose, having great relationships, feeling the omnipresence of love, and living a life you choose—a.k.a., your life "style."

Define your Ideal Lifestyle:

_____
_____
_____
_____
_____
_____
_____

*"Tell me, what is it you plan to do
with your one wild and precious life?"*
—MARY OLIVER

Career/Business

What career and business lifestyle do you REALLY desire? Does your current one bring your frustration or bring your soul alive?

Describe your ideal Career Business Lifestyle? (If you could do ANYTHING you desired.)

_____
_____
_____
_____
_____
_____
_____

What are ways that you can bring your Divine Lifestyle to your career?

_____
_____
_____
_____
_____
_____
_____

HOME

What is your home lifestyle like? Is it filled with love and does it inspire you to live your best life? Remember, unnecessary clutter can take up your energy, whereas something such as an altar or meditation area can bring you clarity.

What is your Home environment like?

_____
_____
_____
_____
_____
_____
_____
_____

What are ways in which you create more room for Positive Energy? (Hint: this usually requires a project that involves purging, clearing out, and letting go of "stuff.")

_____
_____
_____
_____
_____
_____
_____
_____

Love Your Life, Rock Your Passion

Activities

What activities are in your everyday lifestyle? What is your day comprised of? By becoming more conscious of your daily activities, you can see where there is room for improvement for you to stay on your path and flourish. For example, if you find you usually are watching TV while you cook, perhaps having quiet while you prepare a meal will bring you back to the present moment.

What are your daily Activities?

_____
_____
_____
_____
_____
_____
_____
_____

What Activities would you like to add?

_____
_____
_____
_____
_____
_____
_____
_____

PROSPERITY

Take a moment to contemplate in what areas of your life you are prosperous and where there is space for you to open up to greater abundance.

Make a list below of the activities in which you feel prosperous and where you do not.

Where I Prosper in my life:

_____
_____
_____
_____
_____
_____

Where I need to give greater attention to in order to Prosper in my life:

_____
_____
_____
_____
_____
_____

AFFIRM: Money flows to me in increasing amounts consistently over time through multiple sources of income that consist of _____, _____, _____, _____, _____, and I give thanks for all of the abundance in my life now.

Travel

Seeing new places will give you seeds that will allow all areas of your life to bloom. We all know the riches that travel can bring to our lives, but perhaps it seems daunting to consider, given the daily realities of your life. Take small steps to bring your travel plans to fruition.

If you want to travel to Brazil, perhaps start by finding a Brazilian restaurant near where you live. Talk to the people who work there, ask what it is like. Create a vision board with information you find from travel magazines and online. Perhaps take a local class to learn the basics of the language. Sign up for travel deals and alerts for the locations where you want to go.

Open yourself up to new connections and learn about these places so that when you do travel there you will be more than just ready.

Make a list below of all of the places that inspire you and where you hope to travel. By having these places at the forefront of your mind, it will be plant seeds in your subconscious mind.

_____
_____
_____
_____
_____
_____
_____

"I haven't been everywhere, but it's on my list."
—SUSAN SONTAG

Culture

What is your culture like? When you are at home or go out into the world how do you interact? Do you find yourself to be curious and open? Do you live in a male-dominated world? Are those around you free to be open and true to what they believe? Think about the ways that the culture in which you have been exposed to has influenced your life.

Describe below the Culture in which you live:

_____
_____
_____
_____
_____
_____
_____

Think of ways you could create a Culture in your own home, business, or environment in which you would flourish.

_____
_____
_____
_____
_____
_____
_____
_____

Philanthropy

How do you give back to this world? To your community? To the causes that you care about?

Philanthropic endeavors are an important way for you to make your mark on this world. The work you do in this sector may leave you feeling more fulfilled than any other work that you do. Especially if your job does not fulfill your passions, but rather supports you financially, your philanthropic efforts may be the core of your happiness.

What Philanthropic activities are you involved in? In what areas do you serve on a board or in leadership roles?

_____
_____
_____
_____
_____

In what ways can you deepen this involvement?

_____
_____
_____
_____
_____
_____

Time, Treasure, Talent; to those that are given much, much is expected. We ALWAYS have something to give (including kindness, our compassion, our forgiveness and our love).

Resources

Make a list of the Resources that you have at your disposal to assist you on your path to living a bliss-filled and divine life in the here and now.

_____
_____
_____
_____
_____
_____
_____
_____
_____

Add below your favorite books and/or books that you are committed to read this coming year:

_____
_____
_____
_____
_____
_____
_____
_____

Namaste.
—WENDI

Love Your Life, Rock Your Passion

Habits, Rituals, Daily Routines

We are each given the same 24 hours a day.

No one is given any more or any less.

How will I choose to live those 1440 minutes?

24 Hours

Design the ideal day.

What time would you wake up? Let's start there. _____

Next, how would you begin your day?
(Hint: Spending a few minutes in gratitude, hydrating, meditating, etc.)
_____
_____
_____

WHAT IF ANYTHING REALLY WAS POSSIBLE?

Describe what your "ideal morning" would include.
(Remember you get to design this into something that excites you and makes you come vibrantly alive.)

_____
_____
_____
_____
_____
_____
_____
_____
_____

Creating Your Ideal Day

What would you fill your day with?
(Hint: Your ideal career, business, activities, education.)

_____
_____
_____
_____
_____
_____
_____
_____

> Don't forget to include interests such as taking a walk, meeting a friend for lunch, listening to music, or enjoying some quiet time alone.

_____
_____
_____
_____

My Tribe

Who are the people you would interact with throughout the day?
(Remember that you get to pick who you want to add to your life—
they can be cool, hip, and interesting.)

_____
_____
_____
_____
_____
_____

If you could choose any five individuals to spend time with, who would they be?

1. _____
2. _____
3. _____
4. _____
5. _____

Love Your Life, Rock Your Passion

Creating Your Ideal Day

What would your evening routine consist of? Do you make dinner or go out to eat? (Hint: Perhaps you prepare a delicious organic salad or stroll to the local cafe to dine outdoors.)

_____
_____
_____
_____
_____
_____
_____

> It's not happy people who are thankful,
> it's thankful people who are happy.

What are you most grateful for?

_____
_____
_____
_____
_____
_____
_____
_____

1440 Minutes

What is your bedtime ritual?
(Hint: Do you read, write, or listen to music before falling asleep?)

_____
_____
_____
_____
_____
_____
_____

> WE ARE MADE OF ENERGY. THE BODY REQUIRES 7–8 HOURS OF SLEEP EACH NIGHT TO BE THE HEALTHIEST, HAPPIEST, MOST PRODUCTIVE VERSION OF OURSELVES. (JUST SAYIN')

If you could plant one powerful seed of goodness before going to sleep, what would it be?
(Hint: Sending out a prayer for peace in the world.)

_____
_____
_____
_____
_____
_____

Inspiration

Don't look for happiness.

CREATE IT!

The Happy Dream

My Thoughts, Ideas, and Visions for the World

_____
_____
_____
_____
_____
_____
_____
_____
_____
_____
_____
_____
_____
_____
_____
_____

Change can be made in the twinkle of an eye.

Who Do I Admire Most?

When you admire someone it is because the traits you see in that individual are the ones that are most important to you. Think of ten people that fall into that category and you admire most.

This list can include people that you know or people that you don't know, who are either living or have passed. They can be a TV personality such as Oprah, a great spiritual leader like Gandhi, or even your family members.

Name:_____

Character traits: _____

_____

Name:_____

Character traits: _____

_____

Name:_____

Character traits: _____

_____

Name:_____

Character traits: _____

_____

Name:_____

Character traits: _____

_____

Who Do I Admire Most?

Name: _____

Character traits: _____

_____

Name: _____

Character traits: _____

_____

Name: _____

Character traits: _____

_____

Name: _____

Character traits: _____

_____

Name: _____

Character traits: _____

_____

My Timeline

Going backward in time, fill in your highlights and memorable moments. Then, going forward, fill in your wishes, dreams, and desires.

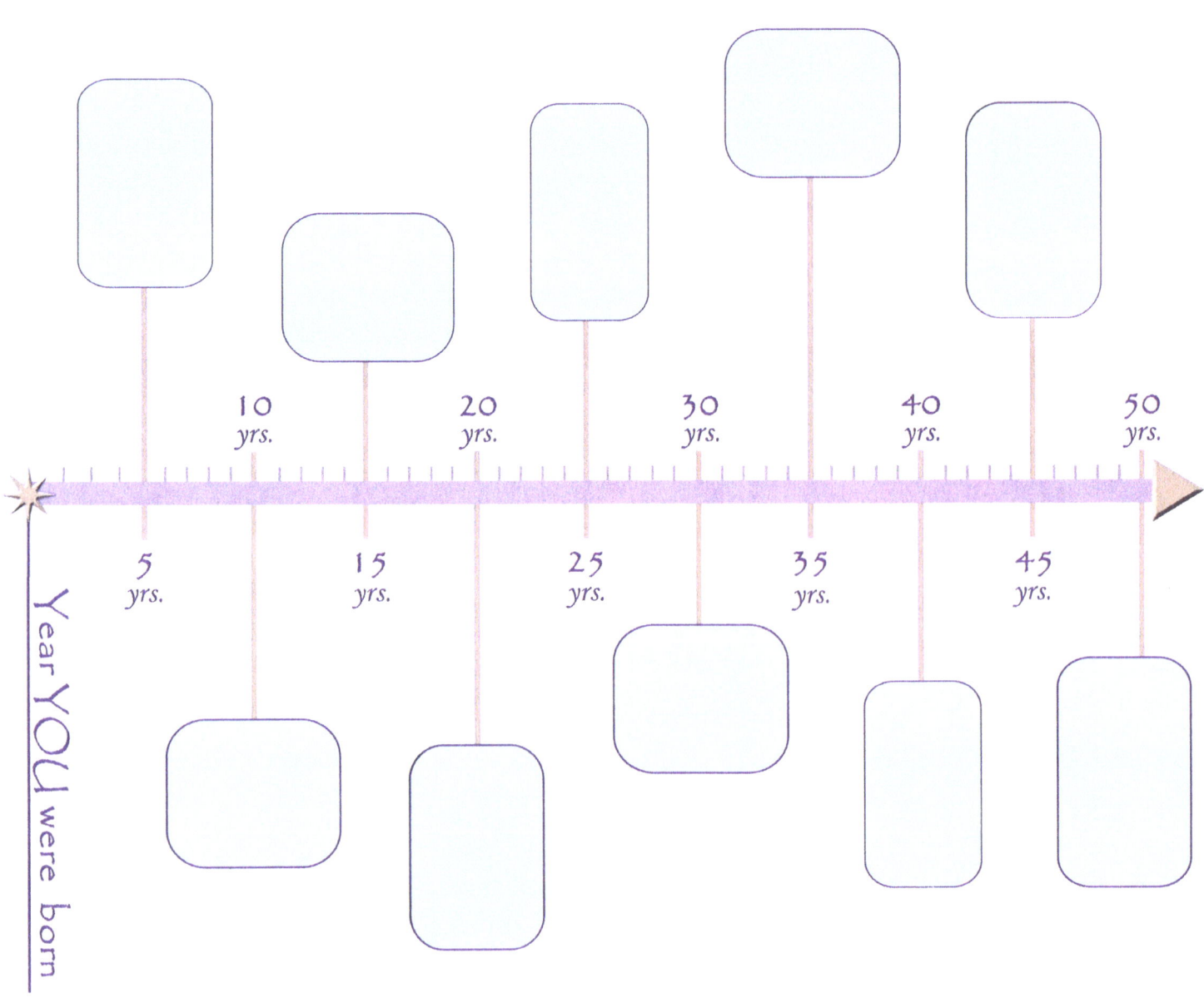

Past... Present... Future

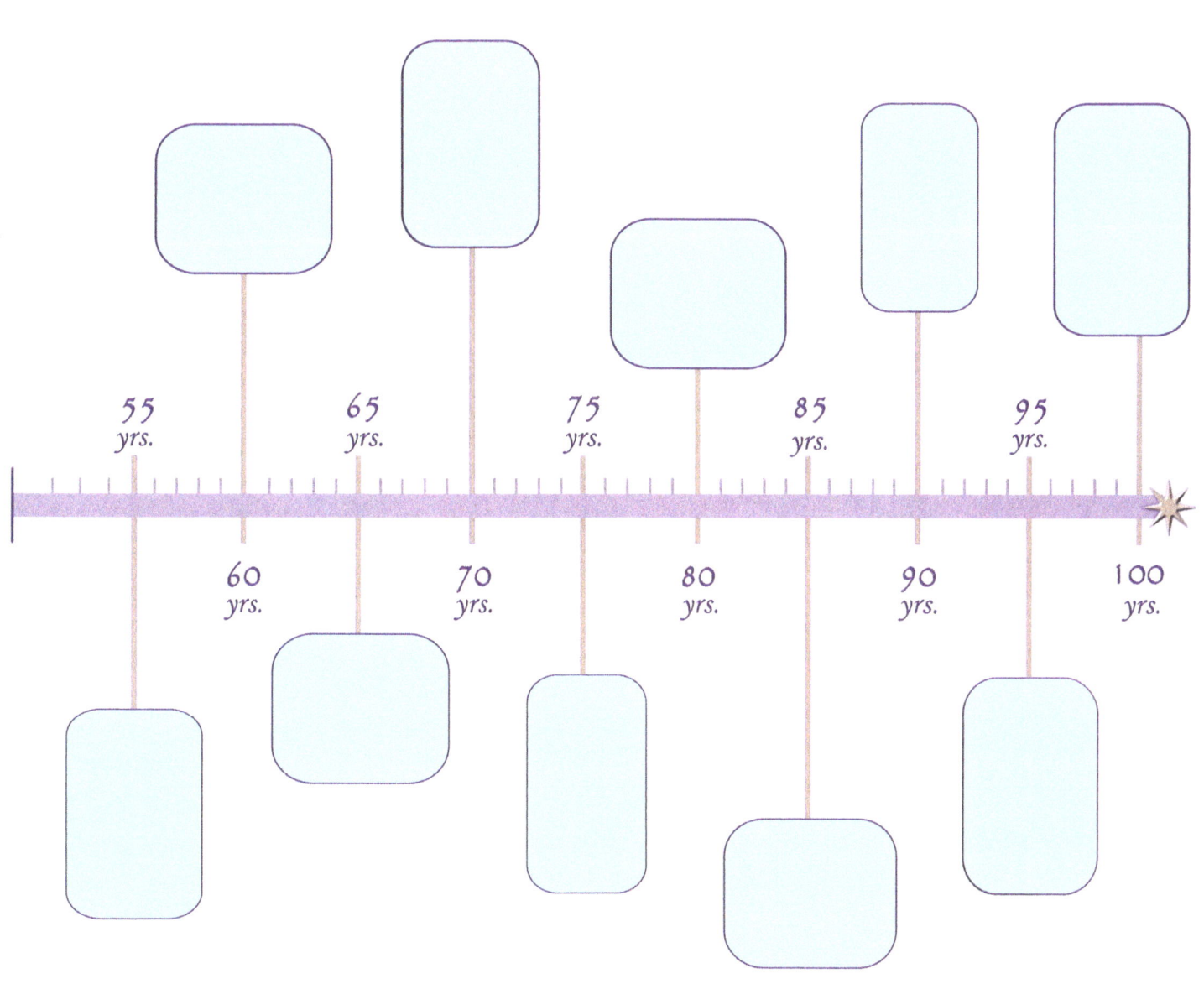

Love Your Life, Rock Your Passion

Note to Younger Self

If the you that you are right now could write a letter to your younger self, what would you say? Use the space below to share your wisdom and insights with your younger self (perhaps you want to share forgiveness, the lessons you have learned along the way, encouragement, and a big dose of powerful inspiration for your future).

Dear _____ (your name)

_____
_____
_____
_____
_____
_____
_____
_____
_____
_____
_____
_____
_____
_____
_____
_____
_____
_____

With acceptance, gratitude, and love,

_____ (your signature)

Inspiration

"The secret to change is to focus all of your energy, not on fighting the old, but on building the new."

—Socrates

The Power of Will

If I were willing, my spirit is calling me to:

_____
_____
_____
_____
_____
_____
_____
_____
_____
_____
_____
_____
_____
_____
_____
_____
_____
_____
_____
_____

Hold it lightly and be guided by your inner wisdom.

Doodle Page

Inspiration

"When I thought I couldn't go on, I forced myself to keep going. My success is based on persistence, not luck."

—Estee Lauder

Your Legacy

Write Your Eulogy

What do you want people to remember about you when you are no longer here?
What words would you like them to use to describe you?
What would you want them to say?
Take some time and give these questions some deep thought.

_____
_____
_____
_____
_____
_____
_____
_____
_____
_____
_____
_____
_____
_____

Love Your Life, Rock Your Passion

Inspiration

"The question isn't who is going to let me; it's who is going to stop me."

—Ayn Rand

Power Words

A   Amazing, Awesome, Abundance, Authentic, Angels, Appreciative, Achievement, Allow, Acceptance, Alive, Art, Awaken, Awe

B   Beautiful, Blissful, Believe, Blessed, Balance, Blossom, Bountiful, Breathe, Bright, Brilliance

C   Calm, Clarity, Compassion, Courage, Creativity, Confidence, Consciousness, Cheerful, Curious

D   Delightful, Divine, Dream, Determination, Dazzle, Delicious, Dynamic

E   Energetic, Enhance, Expansion, Ease, Empower, Effortless, Embrace, Energy, Enjoy, Excitement

F   Fun, Friendly, Focus, Fearless, Freedom, Faith, Frequency, Fantastic, Forgiveness, Full

G   Great, Good, Gratitude, Generous, Giving, Growth, Giggle, Grace, Gentle, Groovy

H   Happiness, Harmony, Hugs, Honor, Humility, Health, Hope, Heal, Humanity

I   Innovation, Inspiration, Integrity Intuition, Improve, Inhale, Invigorate

J   Joy, Jolly, Jubilant, Jump, Jasmine

K   Kindness, Kiss, Kinetic

L   Love, Leadership, Light, Lucky, Limitless, Laugh, Lavender, Learn, Liberate, Listen

Power Words

M   Mindfulness, Mindset, Magnetic, Manifest, Meaningful, Miracle, Music, Majestic

N   Non-attachment, Nurture, Nature, Nourish

O   Oneness, Opportunity, Open, Overflowing, Optimistic

P   Pleasant, Passionate, Prosperity, Powerful, Purpose, Protection, Positivity, Playful, Patient, Peace

Q   Quiet, Quality

R   Relaxation, Resilient, Release, Receive, Radiant, Realize, Reflection, Refresh

S   Strong, Simply, Surrender, Success, Shine, Sincere, Sing, Soft, Sparkle, Special, Savor, Stretch

T   Thankful, Truth, Treasure, Thrill, Tickle, Tolerant, Thrive, Thoughtful, Transcend

U   Understanding, Unique, Us, Unfold, Unshakable, Uplifting, Useful

V   Victorious, Vibration, Visualization, Vitality, Validate, Valued, Vibrant

W   Wonderful, Wealth, Wellness, Warmth, Wonder, Worthy, Whole

Y   Yes, Yoga, Yummy, Youthful

Z   Zest, Zeal

Read this list into a recorder and listen to it before going to sleep at night so that the positive messages are planted into your subconscious mind.

Flourish Reverse Engineering

One Year From Now . . .

Close your eyes and visualize your very best year.

Use words to describe "in reverse" what the year looked like BACKWARDS as if it has already happened.

See your body fit and tone. See a loving relationship with a wonderful life partner. See your home overflowing with love. See adventure and travel. See abundance and prosperity. See an image of yourself laughing, having fun and enjoying life. See success in every area of your life.

What does that look like? Can you describe it like you would describe a movie you have already seen?

Use phrases in the past tense. Use words that evoke emotion with deep feelings of gratitude and fulfillment. Describe details that include your five senses: seeing it, smelling it, feeling it, tasting it, hearing it.

To get started, take your mind forward and pretend it is 12 months from now. Use the starter phrase here:

> It is the last day of the year and this year HAS been _____
> and _____. So many great things have happened like
> _____ and _____. Although there have
> been challenges I have been able to overcome them by _____
> _____.

To truly manifest your desires, remember to add as much emotion and feeling as possible. The subconscious mind doesn't know if something is real or imagined.

Love Your Life, Rock Your Passion

Flourish Reverse Engineering

Now it is your turn to create your ideal future "IN REVERSE."

_____
_____
_____
_____
_____
_____
_____
_____
_____
_____
_____
_____
_____
_____
_____
_____
_____
_____
_____
_____
_____
_____
_____
_____
_____
_____
_____

See the vision.

Flourish Reverse Engineering

Picture the results.

Create Your Life Vision

Reverse engineer it...

Visualize your goals as if they have already happened.